learn *to* SPEAK FASHION

a guide to CREATING, SHOWCASING & PROMOTING **YOUR STYLE**

WRITTEN BY LAURA deCARUFEL
DESIGN & ILLUSTRATIONS BY JEFF KULAK

Owlkids Books Inc.
10 Lower Spadina Avenue, Suite 400, Toronto, Ontario M5V 2Z2
www.owlkids.com

Distributed in Canada by University of Toronto Press
5201 Dufferin Street, Toronto, Ontario M3H 5T8

Distributed in the United States by Publishers Group West
1700 Fourth Street, Berkeley, California 94710

Library and Archives Canada Cataloguing in Publication

deCarufel, Laura
        Learn to speak fashion : a guide to creating, showcasing,
and promoting your style / written by Laura deCarufel ; illustrated
and designed by Jeff Kulak.

Includes index.
Issued also in electronic format.
ISBN 978-1-926973-37-1 (bound).--ISBN 978-1-926973-42-5 (pbk.)

        1. Fashion--Juvenile literature. 2. Clothing and dress--Juvenile
literature. I. Kulak, Jeff, 1983- II. Title.

GT518.D43 2012   j391   C2011-907225-4

Library of Congress Control Number: 2011941966

E-book ISBN 978-1-926973-44-9

Canadian Patrimoine
Heritage canadien

Canada

Ontario
Ontario Media Development
Corporation
Société de développement
de l'industrie des médias
de l'Ontario

Canada Council Conseil des Arts
for the Arts du Canada

ONTARIO ARTS COUNCIL
CONSEIL DES ARTS DE L'ONTARIO

We acknowledge the financial support of the Canada Council for the Arts, the Ontario Arts Council,
the Government of Canada through the Canada Book Fund (CBF) and the Government of Ontario
through the Ontario Media Development Corporation's Book Initiative for our publishing activities.

Manufactured by WKT Co. Ltd.
Manufactured in Shenzhen, Guangdong, China, in November 2011
Job #11CB3016

A   B   C   D   E   F

Owl
kids
Publisher of Chirp, chickaDEE and OWL
www.owlkids.com

For James and my family—L.dC.

For Kelsey and Oliver—J.K.

LEARN TO SPEAK FASHION

STRIKE YOUR POSE!

From the outside, fashion seems like its own universe, doesn't it? A universe already too massive, too perfect, too complete to possibly be a part of.

After all, fashion is full of incredibly talented people creating incredible things: from designers dreaming up amazing clothes to photographers and stylists creating photo shoots for glossy magazines. It's all there. What could you really have to offer?

But guess what? The distance you feel between yourself and the world of fashion is all in your head. In truth, there are all kinds of gaps in the fashion universe that haven't been filled—and they can be filled by people like you.

As a writer, I've talked to lots of major designers, photographers, stylists, and models who have told me that they felt intimidated by fashion as kids. Now they love it. The only way they could kick that fear? By believing they had a voice worth sharing with the world.

If you feel the call of fashion, embrace it. The more you get involved, the more you'll discover. *Let's get started!*

Psst! Over here!
Let's get to know each other.

Hey, I'm Laura! I'm an editor, a fashion writer, and the author of this book. I've been working in fashion magazines for about ten years: I was the senior editor of *ELLE Canada*, then a couple of years ago, my friend Jenn and I started up our own teen webmag called *Hardly*. That doesn't make me the most stylish person in the world, but it does mean that I've been able to see first hand how exciting fashion can be. It's for everyone, whether you're a famous designer or a shy 12-year-old—the age I was when I first became intrigued by fashion. All you need to get started is a flicker of curiosity. Everything else will be your own unique journey!

CHAPTER 1

Express Yourself

What do you think of when you hear the word "fashion"? A designer taking a bow at the end of a runway as the crowd goes wild? A photographer snapping away? A supermodel pouting on the cover of a magazine?

How about your all-time favorite sweater? That sweet pair of sneakers you doodle on your binder? Or how cool your best friend looks on Picture Day?

Guess what? All of these things are examples of fashion. Sure, fashion is about designers, photographers, and models—the "pros." But it's also about everyday clothing, looking at things lying around the house in a new way, and letting your imagination run free! Most important, it's all about you. Fashion belongs to you.

Every morning when you check out your closet and choose what to wear—whether jeans or a leopard print—you're using fashion to tell the world about yourself. What you like. Your attitudes. Sometimes even how you feel that day.

Fashion is instant communication. We form impressions about people based on what they're wearing without even realizing that we're doing it ("She's all in black, so she must be super emo"). We also recognize potential friends based on how they dress ("I love his plaid shirt. Wonder if he likes indie music, too?").

It's easy to miss that connection when a lot of us think of clothing as something to make us, you know, not naked. But it's so much more. Fashion affects how we meet the world, and how the world meets us. Fashion is about expressing who you are. What could be better than that?

Meeting Fashion

So, first things first: What is fashion? When are clothes more than just clothes?

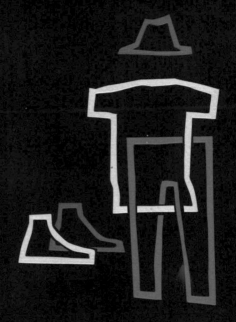

CLOTHES

+ART

=FASHION!

You've got this definition down: Clothes are what you wear to cover your body, everything from your winter hat down to your socks. Easy.

Art is about creating something— a song, a play, a painting—using creativity, skill, and imagination.

Now it gets more complicated. Fashion designers turn straight-up clothes into wearable art. Fashion isn't about making a million pieces that look exactly the same. It's about creating a unique piece that expresses a designer's vision. It's like painting using fabric instead of paint.

YOU ARE AN ARTIST!

So, fashion brings clothes to the next level by treating them like art. But guess what? You can bring your clothes to the next level, too, by making your body a canvas. Personal style—expressing yourself with what you wear—is a major part of fashion. After all, designers are often inspired by what everyday people are wearing on the street. So, go on, turn your Monday-morning school outfit into your own *Mona Lisa*!

Straight Talk

Of course, there can be another piece of the fashion puzzle. A few people in the biz use glitzy phrases that seem too fake to be a part of our real world.

"Sweetie, darling!"
"Absolutely fabulous!"
"Kiss, kiss!"

Help!

Any time you feel surrounded by this sort of chatter, just remember: all of those over-the-top things are just extras, like walnuts in a chocolate chip cookie. Sure, there are people who might like that glamour, others not so much—but whether the walnuts are there or not, the chocolate chip cookie is still a chocolate chip cookie. Fashion is a constant, just like that cookie. For all of those little distractions, fashion never stops being about people and clothes.

FASHION is EVERYWHERE

You're walking down the street, wearing your favorite pair of jeans, when you pass a department store window with mannequins decked out in designer hats and fancy ball gowns. Behind you, a guy in a safety-pinned vest and a pink mohawk rides by on his bike.

So, which of these looks represents fashion?

They all do!

HIGH AND LOW

Just as music can encompass both Beethoven and Kanye West, fashion ranges from street style (like your jeans and the mohawk) to high-end designer fashion (the hats and ball gowns) and everything in between. Everyone uses fashion in their own way. It's an all-you-can-eat buffet where you can pick and choose whatever you want—which is what makes it so much fun to play with!

STREETWISE

One of the biggest influences in the world of high fashion has been the recent rise of street-style photography. You might have seen these photos on the web—pics of real people on the street, in the park or on their bikes, who happen to be incredibly stylish.

BREAKING OUT OF THE BOX

What's new is that the definition of "incredibly stylish" isn't limited to super-tall, super-skinny people wearing head-to-toe designer clothing. All kinds of people and styles are represented: girls in cowboy boots and black-rimmed glasses, guys in three-piece suits and baseball caps, risk takers in feather boas or sequined suits that are so insanely over-the-top they're amazing. The best street-style photography is a reminder of how varied people's everyday clothing can be—and that fashion is literally everywhere! Start thinking of the street as your catwalk, and look for ways to express yourself through your clothes.

CULTURAL EXCHANGE

Clothes are often a huge part of a person's identity. Picture James Bond in a Hawaiian shirt instead of a spiffy suit. Strange, right? Where would Wonder Woman and Spiderman be without their crazy outfits? Or even Rihanna? Their clothes or costumes may be different from each other, but they help define their individual identities—and they're all part of the world of fashion.

YOU THINK YOU KNOW ME...

Irony is a major part of fashion, too—that's when people make fashion statements by wearing the opposite of what's expected of them. Imagine a punk band in preppy polo shirts instead of leather jackets. Sometimes young kids wearing ironic clothes—like trucker hats, oversized round glasses, or ruffled pastel suits from the '70s—can start surprising new fashion trends out of unexpected (even ugly!) items.

Finding Your Style

So, here's a big question: with so much possibility out there, how do you go about discovering your style?

You might have developed your own style already without even really thinking about it (nice!), but if you haven't, don't worry about it. It will probably take some time to find a style that feels right to you. The process of learning what you like best and what best expresses who *you* are is one of the coolest parts of fashion. It's also a pursuit that never has to end—you can reinvent yourself and what you wear whenever you want! What you like wearing now might be totally different from what you like a year from now. As you change, your style will naturally change, too.

NO WORRIES

The most important thing about starting your personal style quest? Let go of your fear. You ever hear that expression "The journey is the destination"? So true! You'll have a great time creating a style mix that's in tune with who you are. So, mess around, experiment! If you normally wear black, try yellow or purple. Add a hat, a tie, a pair of striped suspenders. Getting dressed can be a new adventure every day!

Be Confident

It may be easier said than done, but you'll enjoy clothing so much more if you pay closer attention to what you think rather than what other people do.

> 66 Confidence often starts with shifting your focus a bit. You can walk into a room and wonder what the room thinks of you, or you can decide what you think of the room. 99
>
> —Leith Clark
> **STYLIST AND EDITOR-IN-CHIEF, LULA**

MY STYLE STORY

Do you ever feel intimidated by the idea of breaking out of your comfort zone? I sure did. As a young teenager, I was a total jeans-and-plain-T-shirt kind of girl. I remember seeing a pair of beautiful red Doc Martens in a store and feeling like I couldn't buy them because they were too different from what I usually wore—even if deep down those boots felt more "me" than any of my T-shirts. A few years later—when I felt more confident in myself—that changed. I started experimenting with my look, cutting my hair short and dyeing it red—then black, then blond, then back to red. I spent whole Saturdays at secondhand stores combing through the racks, looking for funny T-shirts and high-waisted jeans from the '50s.

My journey taught me that style is about having the confidence to try new looks—even if remembering some of them makes me laugh now!

Remember: Your clothes don't need to be off-the-wall to have style. You might find that what you like best is a classic look of jeans and a T-shirt. That's cool, too!

Opening Your Eyes

One of the most important steps to understanding any art form is learning how to pay attention. People interested in music listen to many types of songs so they can recognize different instruments and how they sound together. For people interested in fashion, it's all about the eye and learning to look and really see—not just clothes, but everything around them.

I AM A CAMERA

Developing your eye might start with noticing that your best friend looks really cool in a toque, or that you love the way red and yellow fall leaves look together. Nothing is too small to notice. Inspiration is everywhere! It's all in how you look.

LOOK AROUND

Let's practice the art of looking by trying out a mini-experiment. Close your eyes and clear your mind. Now open your eyes, look around for 20 seconds or so, then leave the room. Write down everything that you remember in as much detail as possible—striped orange socks and all. Then go back in and compare your list to what's actually in the room.

Pay attention to what your eye was drawn to—and what it ignored—whether it's the colors of the flowers on your kitchen table or the way the curtains move in the breeze. Developing your observation skills will help you become more imaginative and more in touch with the world around you. The result? You'll have a much bigger pool to draw inspiration from in the future.

Setting the Mood

Your inspiration board will make your heart race every time you see it! You'll experience one of fashion's biggest thrills: the thrill of possibility.

66 I'm always creating boards with the things that I love: color swatches; pieces of vintage wallpaper; photos of women's shoes, hats, gloves, and stockings. And pictures of Rita Hayworth, whom I adore. The constant message? Nostalgia and old-school glamour. 99

—Charlotte Dellal
DESIGNER, *CHARLOTTE OLYMPIA SHOES*

GET ON BOARD!

An inspiration board is exactly what it sounds like: a board covered with a collection of images that you find inspiring. Fashion designers might use one to help focus the mood of their collection. For example, the deep blue of the lake at a designer's cottage could end up being translated into a similar color on a sweater. Or old photos of bands like the Clash could inspire a punk-influenced collection. It's wide open!

ASK YOURSELF: WHAT DO I LOVE?

Your inspiration board is like a road map—you can follow your ideas as they develop. To make one, take a bulletin board or piece of Bristol board and then tape, staple, or glue onto it the things that inspire you. Maybe that's black-and-white photos of a tea party torn from *Vogue* or rock 'n' roll pics of the Beatles in matching suits from *Rolling Stone*. Maybe you like the shade of red on the Kit Kat wrapper—add it! (Um, eat the chocolate first.) You can always create another inspiration board, so let your imagination run free!

CHAPTER 2

Practical Lessons

Personal style? Bring it! Right on! Yeah. Um, wait. How?

Now that you're all inspired and pumped up, where do you go from here? It's one thing to have ideas about what you'd like to wear, but translating those ideas into reality is its own challenge. Maybe you feel a bit lost about what to buy? Or you've fallen into a fashion rut, where you end up buying the same style of shirt or shorts every time you hit the mall? It happens to all of us.

So, how do you kick that and actually create a wardrobe? The number one way to start building your personal style is by experimenting with different looks until you find the ones that work best for you. Think of fashion as a series of building blocks that you're using to create a larger "building"—your wardrobe!

Finding your style often means changing up your ideas along with your clothes, so don't let people's expectations of what you should or shouldn't wear hold you back—and that includes your own. Whether it's a top hat, a tutu, or even just a darker wash on your jeans, push your boundaries a little each time. Just go for it!

Of course, a little specialized knowledge of clothing helps, too. It's amazing how knowing a few basic rules about fit, style, and color will make your fashion journey that much more exciting and worthwhile. That's where experts, like magazine editors and tailors, can bring you to the next level so you can really open yourself up to fashion's possibilities—an understanding of just how those building blocks can fit together.

As you're playing around, ask yourself: What do I feel most comfortable in? What do I look best in? Which pieces make me feel most like myself? Asking those questions—and listening honestly to your own answers—is the key to developing a lifelong friendship with fashion.

WINDOW SHOPPING

Your first step is a fun one: getting out there and scoping the style landscape! You need to know what's on offer before you can make any real decisions, right?

GO-TO GUIDES

Fashion magazines and style blogs are great resources for learning about what's new. That's why a lot of them exist! Their job is to keep track of all the fashion shows and product launches and then feature the best of what comes out of them: the season's top clothes and accessories. A magazine or blog can keep you in the loop about the season's top colors, whether designers are showing boot-cut or flared jeans, and much more!

Of course, you don't need to base your style on what's "in" or copy what everybody else is doing. But knowing the season's trends can start you off with a few new ideas and also help focus your search. Think of trends as suggestions, not rules—you can pick and choose whatever you like!

DREAM A LITTLE DREAM

One of the best ways to understand fashion is to appreciate *zee craft*: that's the technique and creativity behind beautifully made clothes. How? Get as close to fashion as you can.

Get out there and check things out, whether at a department store, designer boutique, mall, or vintage shop.

Look around, touch the fabric, try things on! Forget price tags for now. You're window shopping: daydreaming, not buying, is the point.

Start noticing what you respond to the most. Are there any patterns in what you're drawn to? Certain colors or shapes? Take notes or photos of your faves (just clear photos with the staff first!).

KEEP OUT?

It's normal to feel intimidated by fancy boutiques. A lot of adults are, too. Designer stores often have an air of exclusivity—you know, snootiness—which can make people feel unwelcome. That gets to the heart of an issue that many people have with fashion: it can seem like some members-only club with ultra-snobby gatekeepers. Remember, though, that fashion belongs to everyone, including you! If anyone has an attitude, that's their problem—don't let it be yours.

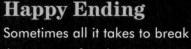

Happy Ending

Sometimes all it takes to break the veneer of exclusivity is to make the first move!

66 When I was 12, I went into the Chanel boutique with my mother. I was so nervous, but the store director was so nice to us! He showed us around, and when we were leaving—after not buying anything, of course—he gave me a press kit with photos of the collection. I looked at it every night for years. 99

—Calla Haynes
FASHION DESIGNER, *CALLA*

Meet Your Body

When it comes to fashion, your body is like a canvas. Just as a painter uses paint to create images, you're using clothes and accessories to create an overall picture with your look. Getting to know your body—and all the different ways to dress it—will help you choose the items that suit you best. Hey, why not create a masterpiece?

HEAD

Since your head is the first thing people see when they look at you, you can make a major statement by dressing it up! The key is not to overdo it—think of items on your head as counting for two items on the rest of your body. So, if you're wearing a statement hat, skip the statement scarf.

What's on it?

Hats: fedora, bowler, beret, tuque, trilby

Other ideas: hairbands, hairclips, bandannas, sunglasses, earrings

NECK

Pieces worn close to your face feel very personal, so your choice of what to wear on your neck communicates a lot about you. Choose pieces that make an impact but don't draw too much attention away from your face. Fashion-wise, your neck's most important job is to frame your face, not overwhelm it.

What's on it?

Scarf: wool, cravat, silk

Other ideas: tie, ascot, shawl, pashmina, necklace

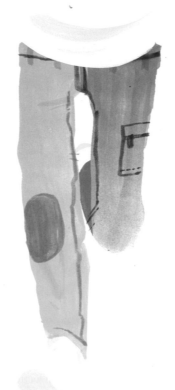
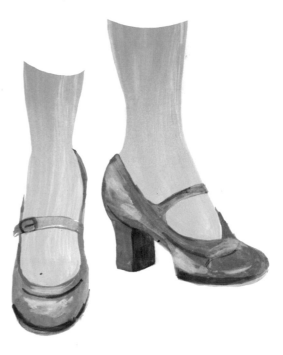

TORSO

Your torso is like the anchor of your look. What you wear on your torso affects what you wear everywhere else, so it's a good idea to make this your first decision when getting dressed.

What's on it?

Sweater: V-neck, pullover, turtleneck, cardigan

Other ideas: jacket, dress shirt, vest, T-shirt, hoodie, tank top, jersey

LEGS

Just as you use your legs to move around, what you wear on your legs is usually pretty functional. You need to wear something, right? Think of your legs as the ice cream in a sundae. They provide the foundation on which to add the more exciting stuff.

What's on them?

Pants: jeans, trousers, capris

Other ideas: shorts, leggings, tights, skirts

FEET

More than any other part of your body, your feet are where you can be totally playful with fashion. Even if you're wearing a conservative outfit, a patterned or brightly colored shoe is like a pop of personality, a wink to other people about who you really are.

What's on them?

Shoes: brogue, sneaker, pump, sandal, boot, ballet flat

Other ideas: socks (as colorful and patterned as possible!)

Building a Wardrobe

As you're building your wardrobe,
peek inside your fridge.

Why? Your fridge and your closet actually have a lot in common. Both of them include day-to-day staples and a few fun extras. That balance is key. You want outfits that you can wear every day and enough options that you can always express yourself in creative ways!

BASIC INGREDIENTS

Your staples are the items that you use or wear all the time. On the fashion front, your life often decides your staples for you. If you're on the soccer team, for example, you're going to need lots of shorts and T-shirts.

Fridge Staples	*Closet Staples*
bread	jeans
milk	T-shirts
mustard	sneakers

STAR INGREDIENTS

Your extras are there to add a little flair. This is where you can incorporate some trendy pieces. It's up to you to decide what they'll be!

Fridge Extras	*Closet Extras*
macadamia nuts	vintage fedora
swordfish	lace dress
caviar	suede moccasins

GREAT GARNISHES

Accessories—like bags, belts, shoes, hats, and jewelry—make amazing extras! Just like spices on a dish. They can be paired with your staples to completely change the look of an outfit. Picture a little black dress with a leopard-print bag, wide belt, and black pumps. Now picture the same dress with a string of pearls and ballet flats. Totally different vibe. You'll have fun playing with accessories!

SHOP TALK

Great style never has to mean expensive style.
Check out these cheap and cheerful wardrobe-building tips.

1. Ask to borrow clothes or jewelry from your family

One of the most reliable things about fashion is that trends keep coming back. In a few months, your older brother's white jean jacket might be the height of fashion!

2. Make regular visits to your local thrift stores

Their stock changes frequently, so there are new treasures arriving all the time. I once happened upon a dress by the avant-garde Japanese designer Issey Miyake at Value Village for $5! So happy! Donate your old clothes, too.

3. Check out vintage shops

"Vintage" technically applies only to clothing that is at least 20 years old, but most shops will have clothes dating back to the '40s and '50s. Amazing for finding totally unique accessories like elbow-length lace gloves or powder-blue suits from the '70s!

4. Host a clothing swap

Invite your friends over, ask them to bring a bunch of clothes that they don't wear anymore…then swap it up! You get a brand-new wardrobe without dipping into your allowance. (Just check in with your parents first.)

How to Dress Well

Experimentation and self-expression rule fashion, but there are a few basic principles that aren't so much about style as they are about overall appearance. Whether your style is funky or preppy, following these tips will help you look your best. Always a good thing!

1. TAKE CARE OF YOUR CLOTHES

The basics: wash them, fold them, hang them on hangers if necessary. Spray your winter boots to protect them from salt. Sew on missing buttons. Use a lint brush—as much as you love your pets, you don't want mounds of dog and cat hair following you around.

2. MIX AND MATCH

Learning a few basic rules about how colors and patterns match will make your style adventures that much more successful. For example...

- Certain colors are "neutrals," which means that they can be paired with any other color. Black, white, and beige are neutrals, and so is denim. You can wear your jeans with anything!

- It's easier to match soft shades than bright ones. And steer clear of matching different shades of the same color, like forest and mint-green.

- When you're wearing multi-colored patterns, try to match one color in the pattern to another main color in your outfit. So, if you're wearing a shirt that has a pattern with purple, blue, and white, choosing a pair of purple, blue, or white pants will look a lot better than introducing a new color, like red.

3. MAKE SURE YOUR CLOTHES FIT

This can be a challenge, especially when you're growing. Fit is also a personal preference: you might prefer shrunken T-shirts while your best friend prefers loose ones. Still, clothes that fit you properly almost always look better than those that are too big or too small.

Point 1: Shoulder

A shirt fits properly when the shoulder seam starts at the end of your shoulder—not halfway to your elbow. When a shirt is too big for you, it makes you look like you're slouching and as though you're bigger than you are. Who wants that?

Point 2: Waist

You should be able to fit one finger between your waist and your pants, shorts, or skirt. Relying on a belt to cinch in your waist will just make the material bunch up. Aim for smooth lines!

Grooming Guide

Get your beauty sleep, wash your face, wear sunscreen, and never underestimate the power of hair.

> 66 Hair helps create icons—think of Marilyn Monroe or Katy Perry. Their hair is integral to their look. But more than anything, having great hair makes you feel good about yourself, while bad hair can ruin your day. Take the time to get a cut that you love, and then take care of it. It's worth it. 99
>
> —Oribe
> **HAIR ARTIST**

Tailor-made

Have you ever tried on a pair of jeans that felt all wrong, then the next pair you tried on felt just right? You can't always tell by looking at something on a hanger what it will look like on you, so always try things on. And here's something to keep in mind: if your clothes don't feel just right, that's the fault of the clothes, not your body. Tailoring your clothes to have them fit as perfectly as possible—whether hemming pants so they're not dragging on the floor or getting your own suit made—will make you look and feel your best. Great tailoring is a key to loving your body as it is.

CHAPTER 3

The Fashion Designer

You're flipping through a fashion magazine, blown away by the awesome clothes and accessories. "Look at the shape of that dress, the color of those shoes! Where do they get all their ideas?"

It's pretty amazing, right? Like a musician creating a song or a poet writing a poem, fashion designers bring something new into the world. They take what was only an idea and make it into something real—so real that you can touch it, try it on, and wear it.

But good design is about more than what you see in magazines. Take a look at what you're wearing right now. Everything—even the most basic sweater or pair of jeans—was designed by somebody. There are many different kinds of fashion designers—those who work as part of a design team for brands like Vans and H&M, and those who design for their own labels or for high fashion houses like Chanel and Lanvin.

Then there are the designers who are still in the doodling stage, or even the daydreaming one. (Hmmm, maybe like you!) Like any artistic profession, fashion design takes time and hard work, but you can kick off the process whenever you want. You don't need to be ready to stage a runway show with 50 looks, or to have perfected your interviews in the bathroom mirror.

All you need right now is to believe that you have a vision worth sharing with the world. It might seem like everything has been done—that every possible idea has been used up. But there is always room for one more voice, one more point of view. And one more great outfit.

ANATOMY
of a
DESIGNER

As a fashion designer, your mission is to:

Create something unique

That will push fashion forward…

Which people will love…

And want to buy.

No problem, *right*?!

Yep, being a designer is a demanding gig that requires a bunch of talents. Let's take a look at all the different roles designers play.

OBSERVER

Designers pay close attention to the world around them. They keep up with what other designers are doing, and also with what's going on all across pop culture. For example, when grunge music hit big in the '90s, the "grunge musician" look quickly spread to fashion. Suddenly, instead of fancy dresses and suits, runway models were wearing Doc Martens and flannel shirts!

TRENDSETTER

How do designers just know that yellow will be the color for spring? Well, actually they don't. Trends are a bit of a mystery. They start off like a suggestion—say, a yellow skirt—and then if enough designers make the same suggestion, it becomes a trend. Designers learn instinctively what suggestions to make and how to push fashion forward.

ARTIST

Like all artists, designers use their creativity to create something new. It's the artist part of a designer that can look at a ferris wheel and think, "That reminds me of a hat!" How designers turn ideas into new clothes is always changing.

HISTORIAN

Once they have their inspiration, designers start researching. For example, if they're inspired by ballet, they'll check out books on vintage ballet costumes. They then discover that ankle-length tutus are made of a lightweight netting called tulle. Now designers can use tulle to create ballet-inspired pieces in their own unique way.

ARCHITECT

You can have the most original ideas in the world, but if they don't fit the body... Just like an architect planning a unique building has to know how the structure will stay standing (and not fall down!), designers need a deep understanding of how clothes fit on the body.

BRAND AMBASSADOR

Even though having imaginative ideas is essential, most designers can't just do whatever they want. Whether they work for high-fashion labels like Balenciaga and Dior or everyday brands like the Gap, if a piece doesn't match the label's style, it's out. Designers need to manage the tricky balance between their own creativity and the needs of the brand.

Early Days

Right now, your interest in fashion might be a flicker or a flame. Either way, you have your own path to follow, so make sure to enjoy yourself along the way!

66 I don't think that it's necessarily fashion that you need to be interested in as a kid, but your own world, music, and the way you live life. Fashion will come when you're ready for it, and then you can apply all that you've learned from life into your work. 99

—Mark Fast
FASHION DESIGNER

Meet Your
muse

Inspiration can come from anywhere you like. That may be freeing, but it can also be puzzling. After all, with so much possibility, where do you start?

How about with a muse? A muse is literally "someone who inspires." Designers—as well as musicians, painters, and other artists—often use a muse to ground their ideas and give them focus. A filmmaker, for example, might have an actor as a muse, and will then write scripts with that person in mind.

STYLE COMPASS

Designers create clothes with their muse in mind. Their muse is like a lens through which they see their collection. If they start straying from their original ideas, the image of their muse brings them back to their central concept.

PICK ME!

Choosing your muse is the fun part. You're looking for someone who you respond to, and who embodies the qualities of your designs. Your muse doesn't have to be somebody you know personally. It could be the singer of your favorite band, or just the cool older kid down the street.

PERSON, PLACE, OR THING

Your muse could also be the cardinal you admire for being so bold and graceful as it stops at your bird feeder every morning. After all, muses capture the *essence* of one's designs—they don't necessarily have to wear them!

DIFFERENT STROKES

You'll likely choose a different muse than your best friend would. But even if you didn't, all designers are inspired in unique ways. They can look at the same thing and have completely different reactions.

For example, a billowing white sail on a ship might inspire one designer to create a dress with a flowing white skirt. On the other hand, you might start with the sail, think about pirates, and end up with a jacket decorated with gold doubloons. Very Jack Sparrow! A third designer might look at the sail and think: Dude, I got nothing. Next!

TALKING FASHION

Fashion is part of creating an identity, and it's also about making a statement. That means designers are always on the lookout for something that will speak to them, and for something that will express what they want to say.

As a budding designer, keep these questions in mind:

What speaks to me?

What do I want to say?

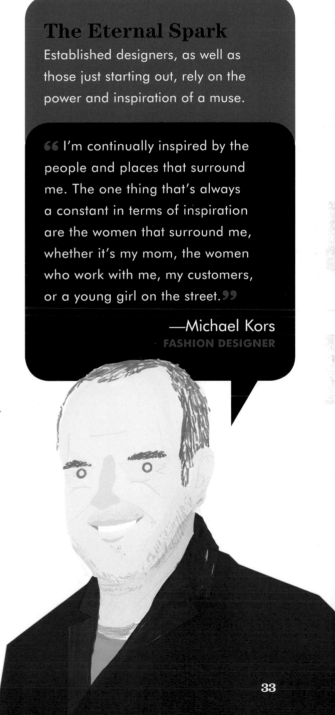

The Eternal Spark

Established designers, as well as those just starting out, rely on the power and inspiration of a muse.

66 I'm continually inspired by the people and places that surround me. The one thing that's always a constant in terms of inspiration are the women that surround me, whether it's my mom, the women who work with me, my customers, or a young girl on the street. 99

—Michael Kors
FASHION DESIGNER

LEARNING HOW TO
Sketch

Sketches are basically rough drawings of your designs. They act as a road map of how to get to your final piece. You can start sketching anytime, but if you're not a natural-born artist, following the tips below will help ensure that what ends up on your paper matches what's in your head.

YOU WILL NEED:

· A sketchbook

· Tracing paper

· A pencil

· An eraser

· A fine-tipped marker

· Colored pencils

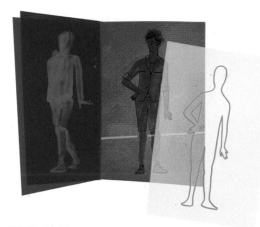

STEP ONE:
Create a Croquis

Say what? A croquis is a figure over which to draw a design. Think of it as a paper doll that you can dress up over and over again. You can download a free croquis online and print it out, or you can make your own by tracing over a figure that you find in a magazine.

Tip: Your figure should have strong lines and a straightforward body position, like a mannequin, so it won't interfere with your design.

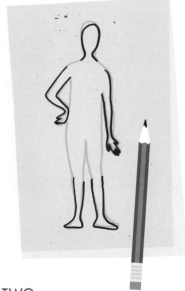

STEP TWO:
Prepare Your Sketch

Put a piece of tracing paper over your croquis, and trace the lines that you know you'll want in your finished sketch, like the head and feet. Or you can retrace the whole figure and plan to erase what you don't need during your next step.

STEP THREE:
Start Your Sketch

Draw your design on top of the croquis.
Remember you can always make
adjustments to your figure by adding
lines or erasing the parts that you don't
need. Consider what type of fabric you'd
like to use and add soft lines to show
texture and movement.

STEP FOUR:
Add the Details

When you're happy with your sketch, place
a piece of paper from your sketchbook over
it and trace the pencil with your marker.
Then shade in your design with colored
pencils or even watercolors! You can also
add patterns and finishing touches—hats,
belts, pockets—to the final sketch.

STEP FIVE:
Remember the Back

Sketch the back of your outfit on a second
croquis. The back is essential! You need a
360-degree view of your idea in order to
really visualize it.

I've Got It!

When you have an idea, get it down as soon
as possible, even if you don't have a croquis
handy. Don't worry, you can always go back
and perfect it later. The spark of inspiration
is what's most important.

Design Focus

Something to keep in the back of your mind when you're sketching:
who are you making this for? Fashion designers can design for
women, men, kids, even pets. You can design clothes, shoes, bags,
jewelry, bathing suits, underwear, socks, hats, ties—phew!
You get the idea: if it can be worn, you can design it.

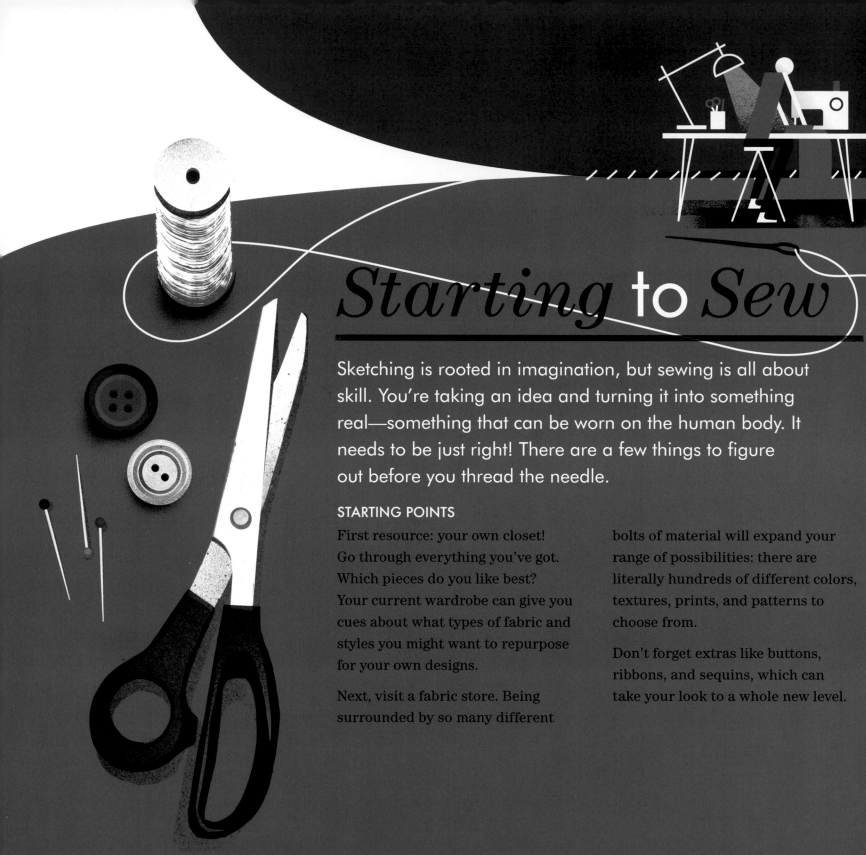

Starting to Sew

Sketching is rooted in imagination, but sewing is all about skill. You're taking an idea and turning it into something real—something that can be worn on the human body. It needs to be just right! There are a few things to figure out before you thread the needle.

STARTING POINTS

First resource: your own closet! Go through everything you've got. Which pieces do you like best? Your current wardrobe can give you cues about what types of fabric and styles you might want to repurpose for your own designs.

Next, visit a fabric store. Being surrounded by so many different bolts of material will expand your range of possibilities: there are literally hundreds of different colors, textures, prints, and patterns to choose from.

Don't forget extras like buttons, ribbons, and sequins, which can take your look to a whole new level.

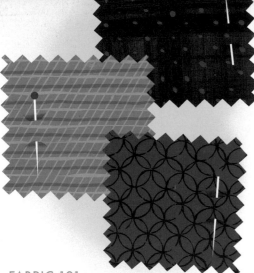

FABRIC 101

If there is a particular fabric that you definitely want to use, ask a store associate to help you find it. These five fabrics are perfect for sewing beginners:

1. Jersey
   Notes: stretchy and soft
   Best for: T-shirts, dresses

2. Rayon
   Notes: easy to dye, hangs well
   Best for: long-sleeve shirts, pants

3. Cotton
   Notes: comfortable against skin
   Best for: shirts

4. Denim
   Notes: sturdy, keeps its shape
   Best for: jeans, skirts, jackets

5. Linen
   Notes: comfortable against skin but wrinkles easily
   Best for: dresses, pants, jackets

TIPS AND TRICKS

1. Take a sewing class
   It makes an enormous difference to have face-to-face instruction for something as hands-on as sewing. Chances are that you have a sewing studio nearby. Check your local listings!

2. Always wash your fabric first
   Imagine the gloom of creating an amazing piece and then having it shrink on you! Terrible. Avoid it.

3. Practice with patterns
   Sewing patterns explain the process of putting together a garment step-by-step. They also include exact measurements for every piece.

4. Double-check all your measurements
   Use your ruler. Sewing is like baking—a pretty exact science. Being off by even an inch can throw off your entire look.

5. Use sharp scissors
   Cutting a straight line is hard enough, but doing it with a dull blade? No way.

6. Don't get discouraged
   Sewing is hard work, but each time you do it, you'll get better. If you feel overwhelmed, stop and come back to it later. It's easy to ruin a piece when you're feeling frustrated.

Learn the Lingo

A sewing dictionary will give you the full scoop, but here's a sneak peek at terms you'll see again and again.

Baste: A stitch that is used to temporarily hold two pieces of fabric together. It's often used in the beginning stages of a sewing project.

Top stitch: A visible row of stitching that acts as decorative flair.

Dart: A fold that creates a curve in the fabric. The darts in a piece are what make it fit.

MAKING YOUR OWN PIECE

When you're just learning how to sew, it's a good idea to start with the basics and save your most creative ideas for your sketchbook. As you develop your skills, you can progress from simple pieces to a perfectly tailored three-piece suit or a dress with a 50-foot train. Sweet!

Since you'll spend lots of time sketching and sewing, let's begin by making a pair of pants that you can wear while on design duty.

YOU WILL NEED:

fabric

elastic

measuring tape

chalk

pins

scissors

a sewing machine

thread

Step 1

Choose your fabric. For comfy pants, jersey, fleece, and flannel are all good bets. If you want a pattern, pick one that looks good when turned in any direction so you don't have to worry about matching up prints. Ask a salesperson at the fabric store to help you figure out the right amount to buy.

Step 2

Measure your waist and the length of your legs. To figure out the width you want for each leg, you can use another pair of pants as a guide.

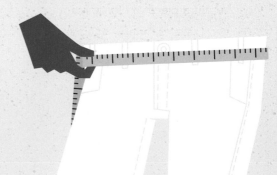

Step 3

Fold the fabric in half length-wise, with the underside of the fabric (the side that will be against your skin) facing up. Create an outline of the shape with a piece of chalk, using your measurements or the other pair of pants. Remember to leave about four extra inches in two places: at the top (near your waist) and at the bottom (by your ankles) for hemming—that's tucking under the fabric and sewing over it to create a straight and sturdy edge.

Step 4

Pinning the outline will help you keep a straight line. Cut the fabric, following your shape.

Step 5

On the sewing machine, sew along the chalk outline, joining the front and back of the pants together. Use thread that matches the color of your fabric as closely as possible.

Step 6

The waist is your biggest challenge! Measure out a piece of elastic that is about two inches shorter than your waist measurement (since you want it to fit snugly). Place the elastic about an inch down from the top of the waist seam, then fold the fabric over it. Sew about half an inch below the elastic.

Step 7

Hem the bottom of the pants by turning up the fabric about an inch and sewing over it.

Step 8

Turn your fabric right side out. Check out your final piece. Nice job!

Tip: Threading your sewing machine is brutal at first, but with practice, it will take you only a few seconds to get it up and running. For quick how-tos, check out videos on YouTube!

EXTREME FASHION
AND
Haute Couture

Have you ever looked at something on the runway and thought, "OK, that's pretty cool and all…but who would actually wear it?"

TOTALLY OUT THERE

Take a label like Viktor & Rolf, which is designed by the Dutch duo Viktor Horsting and Rolf Snoeren. Viktor & Rolf have created coats with 3-D violins sewn into their fronts and shirts that have collars piled one on top of each other so they reach all the way up to the ears!

ABSTRACT AWE

Viktor & Rolf's fashion is obsessed with the extreme—it's often more about pushing the boundaries than creating a realistic wardrobe. But that crazy clothing serves its own kind of purpose. It can be like a fireworks show—simply a beautiful spectacle that makes people smile and gasp. At its best, it can help people think about fashion in a different way. It doesn't always work, but when it does, it creates a totally unforgettable moment.

On the more practical end, such pieces can also attract a lot of publicity for the designers' more "normal" clothes.

GLOBAL FASHION

And what exactly is "normal"? About 98% of the fashion that we see, including most high fashion, falls under the category of ready-to-wear. Just like the name suggests, these clothes are literally ready to wear. Most of the pieces are created in fairly large quantities, so they can be sold in a wide variety of stores all over the world.

HAUTE COUTURE PRIMER

Haute couture is something else entirely. "Couture" is often used as another word for "fashion," but the actual definition is very strict. In France, it's actually protected by law! A group called the Chambre Syndicale monitors who can apply to be considered an haute couture design house. Check out their criteria:

1. You must operate a studio in Paris that employs at least 20 people full time.

2. You must present two runway shows a year in Paris.

3. You must design custom-made pieces for clients, including at least one fitting done directly on the body.

Right now, there are only 11 design houses approved by the Chambre Syndicale. A few of the bigger houses, like Chanel and Dior, have both haute couture and ready-to-wear divisions.

RARE BREED

Unlike ready-to-wear, haute couture is available only to a small group of customers. Why? The pieces typically range from $50,000 to $200,000! The customers are paying to have a totally unique piece and for the detailed craftsmanship. A recent haute couture Givenchy gown needed 1,600 hours of hand embroidery to make it absolutely perfect!

SnapShot

HAUTE COUTURE

Every five years or so, an article appears asking, "Is haute couture dead?" Despite its super-high prices and exclusive nature, couture has a rich history of innovation.

CHARLES WORTH
THE FATHER OF COUTURE

In the 1860s, Charles Worth dressed French aristocracy in gowns with exaggerated silhouettes created by hoopskirts and bustles.

VIONNET
THE INNOVATOR OF COUTURE

In the 1920s, Madeleine Vionnet ditched corsets and bustles in favor of the "bias cut," a diagonal cut that allowed fabric to accentuate the body.

BALENCIAGA
THE ARCHITECT OF COUTURE

From the 1930s to the '60s, Cristobal Balenciaga created exquisitely constructed pieces, sometimes with unexpected touches like ostrich fur! When he retired, one of his countess clients refused to leave her room for three days.

CHAPTER 4

The Runway Show

You've been dreaming about this moment since you started sketching: your first fashion show! Now you're backstage, nervously adjusting a button here, a collar there. Suddenly, you hear the music begin. It's time! You say a little prayer and send your first model down the runway…

It doesn't matter whether you're showing your clothes to fashion editors in Paris or your parents and pet Chihuahua in your living room—hosting a runway show is one of the most thrilling parts of being a designer. It's also where all the elements of the fashion world come together—from behind-the-scenes makeup artists to trend-tracking reporters, everyone is there.

Fashion shows are literally displays of a designer's latest collection. Many professionals work to help the designer realize a particular vision. Stylists accessorize the outfits. Models strut down the runway wearing the clothes. In the audience, photographers, editors, and buyers all crane their necks to record every detail—taking photos and jotting down what they like best.

Awesome yellow dress!

Cool bow tie!

A polka-dot scarf? With that fabric? What a daring choice!

So, your collection is designed and ready. Now all you've got to do is nail the performance part. Let's start with some inspiration from the fashion world!

FASHION as THEATER

Runway shows are about creating a mood that can sweep you up and take your breath away! The clothes are a huge part of that, but other elements—set design, hair and makeup, music, even how the models walk on the runway—all help add to the enchantment. It's just like theater—costumes, lighting, and music come together to complete an overall experience.

THE DEETS

You can put on a fashion show anytime, anywhere, but if you want to know how the professional fashion world handles it, here's a quick overview.

The fashion industry sticks to a schedule where Fashion Week takes place twice a year—designers show their Spring collections in September, and they show their Fall collections in February. Why the long gap?

The collections are like the coming attractions at the movie theater. The gap allows time for editors to feature the clothes in their magazines to get people excited to buy them, and for buyers to carefully choose what they'd like to feature in their stores.

Fashion Week, By the Numbers

2: main fashion show seasons, Spring and Fall

4: major fashion show capitals, New York, Paris, London, Milan

12: shows a day during Fashion Week

50: looks shown in each show

HOT SPOTS

Fashion Week is popping up in lots of other cities, from Montreal to Sao Paulo to Amsterdam. You never know what will be the next major fashion destination. It could be your hometown!

CLOSER TO HOME

Want to check out a fashion show but misplaced the keys to your private jet? (Yeah, me too.) Chances are you can actually see one this weekend: malls and department stores regularly put on fashion shows featuring clothes from their own stock. A bonus: they're free and everyone is invited. Check out your local newspaper or go online to track down the when and where!

SnapShot

SHOW TIME!

A few fashion designers are famous for putting on theatrical shows that the audience looks forward to for months…and then remembers for years afterward!

ALEXANDER MCQUEEN
SPRING 2005: THE CHESS BOARD

Alexander McQueen turned his runway into a giant chessboard and had his models slowly move around it as if they were life-size kings, queens, and rooks. Checkmate!

JEAN PAUL GAULTIER
FALL 2007: THE "COCO MOMENT"

Gaultier's collection featured classic tartans and kilts—and model Coco Rocha doing an Irish jig down the runway! The audience cheers wildly in their seats!

KARL LAGERFELD
FALL 2010: THE ICEBERG

To create a stylish arctic scene, Karl Lagerfeld, the designer for Chanel, actually brought in an iceberg from Scandinavia! Models wearing head-to-toe faux fur walked through the ice and another set that looked like an igloo.

Models:
More Than a Pretty Face

A major must-have for a top runway show? Great models!

Models are the faces and bodies of fashion—their job is to showcase clothes by lending their spirit and energy to a show or photo shoot. Models also often act as muses, inspiring designers, photographers, and editors to new heights. As the designer Yves Saint Laurent once said, "A good model can advance fashion by ten years."

WHAT DOES IT TAKE?

Models need to be on time, enthusiastic, and really hard-working. Sometimes they'll be on a shoot for ten hours, or they'll walk twelve runway shows in one day. Models also need a little something extra, a mysterious kind of spark that is specific to modeling itself. The best models aren't always traditionally beautiful—you could pass some on the street and not really notice them. But in front of a camera, they grab your complete attention. Their appeal is often more about an ability to change their look to fit each shoot than just "beauty."

SAY CHEESE (OR *FROMAGE*)!

For your first show, you'll likely be asking your friends to be models. You can have fun practicing the "model walk" by placing one foot directly in front of the other and looking just a little ticked off. And don't forget these three "classic" fashion poses—you'd be surprised how often you see them in magazine photo shoots. Now let's get posing!

1 The "what's on my shoe?"

2 The "oh, my tummy!"

3 The "white bread or whole wheat?"

Tough Talk

The modeling industry has gotten a lot of well-deserved flak for its narrow definition of beauty. Most models, male and female, are very tall, very skinny, and have white skin. Now think of all the people in your life: how many of them fit into this definition? Exactly. But there are also models who challenge these standards of beauty to include different ethnicities, body types, and so-called imperfections. Look at these examples:

1970s: Lauren Hutton's gap-toothed smile becomes her trademark—despite her agent asking her to fix it.

1990s: Eve Salvail's shaved head and dragon tattoo rocks the modeling world!

2010s: Arlenis Sosa breaks the color barrier when she becomes the first black model to score a multimillion-dollar cosmetic contract.

In Her Own Skin

After struggling with an eating disorder, model Crystal Renn decided to embrace her natural shape. She became famous as a plus-size model, and eventually was a star in mainstream modeling, too.

> **"** I used to compare myself to other people and feel that I always needed to be just a bit skinnier to be worthy of love and attention. It's taken me a long time, but I've learned to love myself for who I am. Trust me: you'll be a lot happier if you do, too.**"**
>
> —Crystal Renn
> **MODEL**

LET'S GET THIS SHOW ON THE ROAD

It's time to go for it and plan your own fashion show! Remember, your first show doesn't need to feature a chessboard or an Irish jig to be amazing—your awesome designs will take care of that!

30 DAYS TO SHOWTIME

This is your checklist to nail four weeks before your show:

- **Location:** Where you're going to have your show

- **Set design:** What extras you'll add to jazz it up

- **Budget:** How much it's all going to cost

- **Team:** Who can help you have the best show possible

LOCATION, LOCATION

Where to show your collection? Think (really) local: your backyard, a hallway in your house, or the sidewalk out front. Also check out neighborhood cafés and galleries to see if you can use their space after hours and if there's a rental fee.

TIP: Don't forget! You'll need folding chairs for your guests, and some "backstage" space for hair and makeup and for your models to get changed.

SET DESIGN

Think about what you can add to your show to make it special. Maybe you'd like to put a daisy on each of your guests' seats or have a screen at the back of the runway with your name on it!

TIP: The set is there to enhance the mood of your collection. A leopard-printed catwalk might be awesome, but if it clashes with your clothes, nix it.

Teamwork

Your team is crucial to success! You'll be swamped the day of the show, so you need people you trust to fill these three roles.

1. STYLIST

The stylist's job is to amp your collection to the max for your show. That means adding accessories—shoes, belts, bags—that complete the look.

TIP: You can always supplement your designs with clothes that are already in your closet—or your friend's closet. Remember: Accessories should add to your beautiful creations, not steal their glory.

2. HAIR AND MAKEUP ARTIST

This person needs to figure out what look will best suit the mood of your collection. When in doubt, keep it simple. If you're showing classic white suits, adding kaleidoscopic hair extensions will distract the audience from what they should be focusing on: the clothes!

TIP: Keep things unified to create an overall vision. If one model has a braid, the next model should, too.

3. MODELS

"Are you a model?" Time to flatter your friends! Chances are, they'll be thrilled to be asked—and to wear your amazing creations!

TIP: Get as many people together as you can. It's more fun, and it will make the show last longer.

The Cost of Style

Fashion shows are usually free to attend. You'll likely have to spend some of your own money to put on the show, even if everyone is volunteering their time and the venue is your front lawn. Do a tally of your potential costs—transportation, daisies, projector, emergency cookies—so you know what you're looking at. You might need to earn some cash to swing it, but it'll be worth it!

EXTRA, EXTRA

You'll be spending the show backstage (until your bow!), so visualize the whole shebang in advance. Do you need someone at the front to let people in and another to show them to their seats? It's better to have too many people helping than not enough.

Almost There!

You've got your location locked down and your team in place. Excitement is building as everything starts to come together!

14 DAYS
TO SHOWTIME

Now it's time to focus on the extra touches that will really bring your show to the next level! Here's your checklist for two weeks before the curtain opens:

- Guest list: Who you want to come
- Playlist: Your show's soundtrack
- Run-through: The order of your looks
- Dress rehearsal: Enough said

RSVP...PLEASE!

Who to invite? Draw up a list of people, then send them an email, or even nicer, send a paper invitation with all of the details: when, where, plus your email address in case they have any questions. Send the invite now, and then send a reminder the week of the show.

Tip: Ask your guests to bring their cameras so they can be your photographers! Of course, you can always tip off the paparazzi, too...

ADD TUNES

A great playlist will help complete the mood that you're going for, and it will also energize your audience, your models...and you. (After all the work you've put in, you might need it!)

Tip: Keep your sound system in mind—you might need to sync an iPod to different speakers around the room to get a truly bombastic sound!

Sounding Board

When making your playlist, stick with one musical theme—your soundtrack should match the mood of your collection as closely as possible.

> ❝ I think about my runway show playlist as being an extension of the woman I'm creating the clothes for. I think, 'What would she listen to?' That's always my starting point. ❞
>
> —Jonathan Saunders
> **FASHION DESIGNER**

ORDER, PLEASE

Just like your playlist, your runway looks should flow smoothly from piece to piece. These three tips will set you on the right path!

1. Start with a bang! Always open the show with the design that you feel best represents your collection.

2. Group pieces together based on color, pattern, and style. If you have a series of short dresses, have them follow each other so they support the same message.

3. Your last look is crucial, too! Designers typically save their most formal outfit for the very end.

Tip: Create printouts of the looks in the order that they appear—like "Look 14: Navy suit"—and have someone distribute them to the audience before the show so they can follow along. This list is called "The Credits." It often includes some words about the inspiration behind your collection.

INSIDE *a* RUNWAY SHOW

Oh, the buzz of a fashion show! Shows are divided into two main areas: the backstage and the runway. Let's take a closer look at how everything comes together.

① ENTRANCE

The audience comes in, stopping to make sure that their names are on the guest list. They need to be on the list to get in!

② FRONT ROW

Reserved for an array of important fashion people— big-name editors, buyers, bloggers—these are the best seats in the house. Celebrities get front-row dibs, too.

③ OTHER ROWS

The rest of the space is filled with other fashion writers, boutique owners, and friends and family of the designer.

④ CATWALK

This is where the models strut their stuff, and also where designers come out to take their bow after the show!

⑤ PHOTO PIT

Before the show, photographers snap pics of the audience. Once the show begins, all their attention is focused on what's on the catwalk.

⑥ THE CURTAIN

The backstage area is dominated by the designer. His or her job is mostly finished, but there's always time for last-minute adjustments—and just a few (or 147) nerves.

⑦ COUCHES

Models read or listen to their iPods while they're waiting for wardrobe and hair and makeup.

8 HAIR AND MAKEUP STATIONS

Armed with tubes of lipstick and cans of hair spray, the hair and makeup artists busily create the beauty looks.

9 CLOTHING RACKS

The collection is organized by outfit, including shoes and accessories, so that models can do lightning quick changes during the show.

10 DRESSING AREA

Stylists help dress the models, while the designer gives them instructions on how to walk and whether to look totally serene or totally grumpy.

SHOW TIME

Everything is all set—the audience is seated and the models are backstage dressed in your collection. Time to hit "play" and get on with the show! So, why do you want to put on a fake mustache, sneak out the back, and catch a bus out of town?

NERVE CENTRAL

It's actually the most natural feeling in the world. Of course you're going to be nervous just before your show. After all, you're letting people see something that you've spent hours and hours working on—that's scary no matter who you are and how many collections you have under your belt!

That's not helping? Sorry! How about keeping these three things in mind:

People are on your side

Including me! You should be proud of yourself for designing a collection and for staging a show. It takes a lot of guts!

Mistakes happen

Don't worry if the music screws up, or if a model walks off without her hat or even trips and falls down. All of those things happen pretty regularly in professional fashion shows, too. It's normal!

There's always the next show

Sure, it seems life and death now, but you'll be working on your next show in no time! Enjoy this experience and learn from it as much as you can.

Now visit the bathroom for the fifth time, take a deep breath, and hit it!

HOW DO I LOOK, COACH?

Your job is finished...almost. Backstage, you're the coach. You speed things along or slow things down if you need to. You make sure that every model looks exactly the way you want before she heads out on the catwalk.

And guess what? Before you know it, it will be over! So much time goes into creating everything—the outfits, the beauty look, the guest list—but fashion shows are over in a flash. The model walks down the runway, poses, then walks back. The whole thing takes 10 minutes max!

After the last outfit, come out and take a bow.

Now bring your team out so that everyone can get some applause.

You've all earned it!

Help!
Having a last-minute bout of why-am-I-doing-this? You're in good company—famous designers experience the same feeling.

> 66 I always get nervous before a show, but I tell myself that whatever happens, it's never do or die. It doesn't have to be the ultimate show because there is always another show. 99
>
> —Jeremy Laing
> **FASHION DESIGNER**

CHAPTER 5

The Fashion Shoot

You're behind the camera, snapping away, as your model poses in time to the song you're blasting. "Smile! Now look bored. Yikes, that's too bored! Wait, that's it! PERFECT." Snap!

Photo shoots are one of the most exciting parts of fashion. A team—photographer, fashion editor, model, stylist, hair and makeup artist—comes together to create images for magazines, ad campaigns, billboards, or even just for fun!

Some shoots can be major operations. A 20-page Alice in Wonderland spread that appeared in *Vogue* featured a model dressed as Alice, fashion designers playing the parts of the Mad Hatter and the Red Queen, a real baby pig, fake flamingos, and six-feet-tall papier mâché mushrooms! The total number of people who made the shoot happen? Forty. Yowza.

Of course, shoots can also be totally low-key: like a model in a white shirt sitting on a chair. Or your best friend carrying a picnic basket through the park. How big or small you make your shoot is up to you. The main thing is that everything—from the team you choose to the clothes you feature—needs to be spot on. You're creating a vision and everything needs to add to it. You might not have access to a baby pig, but it's never too early to start nailing the details.

Your mission? To have people look at your shoot and think, "WOW." As you plan the shoot, think about the fashion photos that have given you a special thrill. What did you like best about them? What set them apart? Now let's talk about creating your own "WOW"! Ready?

Picture It!

A photo shoot tells a story in pictures—just like your family photo album tells the story of your vacation last summer. Like a runway show, a photo shoot should create a complete mood that draws people in and transports them while also showcasing the season's latest clothes.

IDEA CENTRAL

Where to start? With an idea! Photo shoots, like fashion design, can be inspired by absolutely anything: a runway trend, a color, a movie, even a writer. There's no such thing as an idea that's too weird to work—I've seen photo shoots that have been inspired by fairy tales, an oil spill, even strawberry shortcake (sweet!). But whatever the concept is, it still needs to speak in some way to the clothes being photographed.

OFFBEAT INSPIRATION

I once worked on a fashion shoot inspired by all kinds of air travel—planes, hot air balloons, spaceships.

The idea was that the wide variety of that season's summer clothes could be worn nearly anywhere. Rather than recreate the travel sets in a studio, our fashion editor asked different illustrators to draw the backgrounds. We shot the model separately, then added her into the illustrations: waiting in a crowded airport wearing a sundress, soaring above a city in a hot air balloon with her scarf flying behind her, using her tennis shoe to sift the red sand of Mars. What could have been totally cheesy turned into a lovely, imaginative shoot.

BACK AND FORTH

Photo shoots are all about teamwork and bouncing ideas around until you find the right fit. The idea for a photo shoot usually originates with a fashion editor at a magazine or a photographer. Let's listen in on their conversation:

Fashion editor: We want to show a group of friends hanging out together, wearing the season's latest boho clothes—cowboy boots and fringed vests. The idea needs a little something special, though....

Photographer: What about shooting it at a cottage? We could do a "day-in-the-life" story, with photos by the water, at the barbecue, against the sunset!

Fashion editor: LOVE IT!

Don't be afraid of talking through ideas with a friend you trust. Most of the best ideas are formed this way—besides, you don't need to do everything yourself!

Magic Moments

The behind-the-scenes of a shoot can be as much fun as the resulting photos. Natalia Vodianova remembers embodying Alice for *Vogue*'s Alice in Wonderland story.

"The set felt like a film. We shot over three days with a whole cast of people—Donatella Versace; Rupert Everett, who kept reciting poetry; designer Tom Ford, who showed up in perfect white suit and gloves, and then was instructed to hang upside down for hours to look like he was flying into the rabbit hole. To make the picture work, he did it."

—Natalia Vodianova
MODEL

On the Shoot

A great team is essential for a great shoot. You're looking for people who are flexible enough to work well together while also being committed to a specific vision. It's a tricky balance, but when it works, it's magic! Let's meet the main players.

PHOTOGRAPHER

Yep, the photographer takes the photos—but the job is way more complex than just pressing a button. The photographer often works beforehand with the fashion editor to develop the shoot's concept. At the shoot, he or she gives direction and encouragement to the models. An experienced photographer also gives the shoot its look by using different lighting and lenses.

FASHION EDITOR

The fashion editor's job is to oversee the shoot and make sure that all the elements come together. Which can mean being a pain in the neck! "How about snapping from this angle?" "Let's make the lipstick plum for this shot." "Where did that puppy go?" It's a bit like being a coach—the trick is to manage everything while still giving the rest of the team the freedom to do their jobs.

STYLIST

The stylist chooses a (big!) selection of clothes and accessories, then pairs them together to create specific outfits. During the shoot, the stylist is always making sure that the outfits look perfect. This means straightening hems, pinning shirts and dresses that are too big, and lots and lots of lint rolling.

HAIR AND MAKEUP ARTISTS

The hair and makeup artists (often two different people) work together to create a beauty look for the shoot. They work with the fashion or beauty editor at the magazine to come up with a vision for the hair and makeup that will enhance the story being told in the photos. Then they set to work creating it on the day of the shoot. Often, this can be several different looks, or new ideas are suggested and tried on the spot. They always need to be ready to improvise!

MODEL

The model's job is to capture the essence of the shoot, whether it's bright and funny or dark and brooding. A great model can use his or her spirit and personality to bring the photos to life!

PHOTOGRAPHER'S
CORNER

Taking pictures is a snap, but learning how to take *great* pictures requires time. The good news is that by learning a few basics, you'll get better really quickly.

FOUR SUPER-EASY STEPS TO BETTER PHOTOS

1. EXPLORE!

Check out magazines, blogs, and photography books to see what kind of style you're most intrigued by. Do you like black-and-white photos? Street-style pics? Something else? You're looking for ideas for your own pictures.

2. BRING A CAMERA EVERYWHERE

At school, at the park, on field trips—take pictures of everything. Perhaps you thought you liked shooting objects most, when you actually prefer photos of people. Either way, you'll start understanding what makes a great photo. Just get permission from people before taking their photo.

3. MAKE A PLAN...

Know what you're hoping to get out of each picture. Do you want a close-up or full-length shot? A moody side profile or eye contact with a big smile? Visualizing the photo in advance will make the shot better—and help you feel more sure of your skills.

4. ...BUT ALSO BE SPONTANEOUS!

Remember: you can change your plan if you want. If an idea grabs you, go for it! Some of your most memorable photos will come after you've said, "I know it sounds crazy, but how about this?"

EYE

As in: "She has a great eye."

What it means: Understanding what makes a good photo and great photo opportunities.

What it means to you: You develop your eye the same way you do your "look list" back in Chapter 1—by observing things around you.

SELECTS

As in: "I'm making my selects right now"

What it means: The very best photos from a shoot. After a shoot, the photographer makes the first round of selects, which the fashion editor edits down further.

What it means to you: You make selects, too: when you choose to delete a fuzzy picture or keep one in which everyone has their eyes open.

BOOK

As in: "Wow, your book is looking amazing."

What it means: The photographer's portfolio: a collection of his or her best shots.

What it means to you: You can create your own book—either online in a blog format or by printing out the photos that you like best and putting them in an album.

SnapShot

PHOTO FINISH

Fashion photography changes almost as frequently as fashion itself! The most consistent trend has been to move away from formal compositions to a more relaxed style.

HORST P. HORST
STUDIO MASTER

Back in the 1900s, Horst created elaborately staged tableaux, usually in black-and-white, where the main focus was on the clothes: the lace on a shawl or ribbons on a corset.

RICHARD AVEDON
ENTER MOVEMENT

In the 1940s, Avedon introduced energy and spontaneity. His models laughed, jumped, even danced!

GARANCE DORÉ
STREET STYLE

In the 2000s, Doré's portraits of stylish—but everyday—people on the street helped start an era of more laid-back photography.

Stylist Zone

Chances are, you already know a ton about being a stylist. After all, you are one, with a very special client: you!

The choices you make about what to wear when you get dressed every morning are just like the choices a professional stylist makes on the job: This blue T-shirt or that yellow one? With a belt or without? A stylist just does it on a bigger scale—and for other people. Here are the three main ways that they spend their days:

1. Sourcing Clothes

Stylists spend a lot of time window shopping, scoping out the best possible clothes for shoots. They visit designer studios, build up a list of favorite shops to borrow clothes from, and create relationships with store owners. That way, if they're looking for purple shoes—or something more obscure, like an 18th-century wig—they already know who to call.

2. On Set

In addition to working on shoots, stylists also help "dress" actors for movies and TV shows. For these gigs, they're called "costume designers," but the idea is the same: every outfit needs to be specifically chosen to add to the storyline. Whether for a kid playing soccer on a sitcom or the lead in an indie film, stylists put together clothing that suits the scene.

3. (Working) On the Stars

Celebrities look so perfectly put-together that it's actually kind of weird—you never see someone famous walking around with a mustard stain on their shirt. How do they do it? Easy! They have a whole team of people whose job it is to make them look great, including a "personal stylist" who puts together outfits for all their parties, movie premieres, or concert tours.

BEHIND THE SCENES

The next time you're at the grocery store, browse through a few magazines that have big photo shoots, like *ELLE* and *Rolling Stone*. One of the secrets of the fashion world is just how much goes into making the final shots look absolutely perfect, from lots of lighting to hours of hair and makeup.

THE REAL DEAL

"Perfection" is a fantasy that makes for beautiful photos, but it's not real. Remember that when you're looking at fashion images, and when you're thinking about yourself in relation to fashion—you don't need to be perfect either.

Reality Check

Styling may look like a glamorous gig, but the behind-the-scenes is all about the details—and being prepared for anything.

> 66 I'm always reminding myself the moment I get careless—like putting my pen in the pocket of a bag with some merchandise—that will be the day it explodes and ruins thousands of dollars of designer pieces. I'm in constant preventive action, trying to avoid the worst-case scenario for everything and anything. 99
>
> —Erin Stanley
> **STYLIST,** *JUDY INC.*

DIY SHOOT

Now it's time for the best part: creating your own shoot! It's totally up to you how big or how small you want to go. These steps will help direct your path.

STEP ONE
Brainstorm Ideas

What kind of shoot would you like to create? What's inspiring you? Do you want to shoot inside or outside? A mix of both? What kind of mood do you want to create—happy and upbeat? Or seriously emo?

STEP TWO
Assemble Your Team

Get your friends, brothers, sisters, neighbors (and pets?) together and see who is interested in doing what: photographer, stylist, hair and makeup artist…you've got the list! At first, you might need to pull double duty (do a few different jobs), but that's the best way to learn and figure out which job is your fave.

STEP THREE
Be Creative

Like, really creative. Go through every closet you can to see what could be the "wardrobe" for the shoot. Visit garage sales to check out cheap possible props. Figure out the best way to ask your older sister if she'll let you borrow her makeup. (May the force be with you!)

STEP FOUR
Remember the Small Stuff

If you're going to take over the basement for two days, clear it with your parents first. Don't forget about snacks—they're essential brain food! When you're working for *Vanity Fair*, you can have the shoot catered with frogs' legs (or…not), but when you're just starting out, you're on sandwich duty. Apples, granola bars, and lots of water will also help keep everyone's energy levels up.

STEP FIVE
Create a Shot List

This is a numbered list of the photos you want, in the order you want them taken. It will help you figure out the story you want to tell and make the shoot go faster and smoother. Always a good thing!

STEP SIX
Get Out There!

You'll never feel 100% prepared, so take a deep breath and go for it. Have fun, and be patient with your team. You'll learn lots together if you let yourself make a few mistakes.

HOW WAS IT FOR YOU?

Fun? Well, start planning your next shoot! Hopefully your first one went great, but the best way to continue learning and getting better is to keep going.

A FASHION SHOOT PLAYLIST

Hey, don't forget a stereo. Good tunes will keep you going when your energy starts to flag. These are my three favorite fashion shoot songs— you'll have fun discovering yours!

THE CLASH "Hitsville UK"

MADONNA "Get into the Groove"

THE KILLS "Sour Cherry"

inside a FASHION MAGAZINE

Magazines are responsible for some of the biggest and most striking photo shoots in fashion.

Their editors profile designers in articles, attend runway shows, and create lavish shoots to showcase the designers' clothes. Being mentioned in a big magazine like *Vogue* or *ELLE* can totally transform a designer's career. So, as you can imagine, working at a fashion magazine is an exciting and influential job!

You may be years away from a full-time gig, but it never hurts to get the scoop on the details. It might also give you a new understanding of, even appreciation for, how all those mags on the newsstand get there.

WORDS AND PICTURES

The team at a fashion magazine is divided into two parts: the editorial team, a.k.a., the word people, and the art team, a.k.a., the picture people.

Let's get to know them!

1. The editorial team includes—you guessed it—the editors. But what's an editor? Editors are responsible for all of the words in the magazine—they write stories and also assign other stories to freelance writers (those are writers who don't work at the magazine). Then they edit (or correct any mistakes in) the stories that come in. On photo shoots, editors work with the art team, photographers, and stylists to come up with a concept.

2. The art team is overseen by the art director, who is responsible for the overall look of the magazine. The art director guides graphic designers, who then create the layout for articles and photo shoots. They literally decide how each page should look—where the words should go, how big the photos should be, what colors should be used, and so on. If you're saying "ooh" as you flip through a magazine, you can thank the art team!

Go, Team!

My favorite thing about being a magazine editor? The thrill of working with other people to create something great! Sure, it can be tough—everybody has different opinions, and they don't always mesh. Ultimately, though, that's what makes it so rewarding: when it works out, you get the best of everyone's ideas. You probably have moments like that, too—when your English group gets into a groove and puts on a fantastic presentation, or when your soccer team pulls together and comes back from 1–0 to win the game! It feels pretty wonderful to be part of a team that you believe in.

Like, OMG

Fashion writing is sometimes dismissed as being superficial or silly. Don't ever feel embarrassed about being interested in reporting on fashion—or anything else, for that matter.

66 Fashion journalism is no different than any other kind of journalism. It requires detective skills, intelligence, humor, and a literary style. 99

—Nathalie Atkinson,
REPORTER AND STYLE EDITOR,
CANADA'S NATIONAL POST

Laura's Total Recall

During my magazine career, I've been lucky to work on some amazing photo shoots. These are my top three memories (so far!).

THE FIRST ONE

I was fresh out of university when I landed my first job at a fashion magazine called *The Look*. The first shoot I worked on was a major one: we were shooting one model in six different locations—including a café, an art gallery, and an auction house—in one day. Yikes! It didn't help that I was beyond clueless. My job was to act as an assistant to whoever might need help. The stylist asked me to steam a dress for her, but beyond plugging it in, I didn't know how to use the steamer and I was too shy to ask. The fashion editor asked me to order lunch. Somehow I wound up ordering one pizza and two salads for 10 people. Despite, well, *me*, the shoot went smoothly...and I kept my job. The experience made me realize how important it is to speak up. It's so much better to look a little silly by asking a question than to look a lot silly by having to run to a pizza shop and frantically buy up all the slices!

THE BIG ONE

I was lucky enough to work at Toronto's *FASHION* magazine during its special 30th-anniversary issue. To celebrate, the team planned a major shoot: 20 pages of models who had appeared in *FASHION* over the years. My job was to write the story that introduced those pages, which meant tagging along to the studio and observing the scene and its players—models, stylists, photographers, hair and makeup artists, fashion editors—as they made the magic happen. The studio looked like something out of a movie: racks of clothing along one wall, a big table with nothing on it but fresh fruit. A stylist with pins in her mouth fixing a dress. Models drinking bottled water through straws so they didn't ruin their lipstick. It was majorly glamorous and totally unforgettable!

THE SMALL ONE

There's nothing like the thrill (and terror!) of working on a shoot for your very own magazine. The first shoot that my co-editor Jenn and I did for *Hardly* was as DIY as it gets. The location? Inside a friend's soon-to-be-opened café. (People kept walking in, trying to buy coffee!) The photographer and hair and makeup artist were also friends who were kind enough to give up their Saturday afternoon. The model wasn't a professional model at all, but a lovely high school student we'd spotted in a vintage shop. Jenn and I acted as the stylists, fashion editors, DJs, you name it. We baked banana—cinnamon muffins, brought our own books to act as props, and played foosball in between takes. It was a great reminder that being on a photo shoot can be so much fun—and that it doesn't need to be a major operation to organize. That's good news for you, too!

CHAPTER 6

The Biz

Design a collection. Check! Make the clothes. Check! Put on a fashion show. Check! Dude, are we there yet? Almost! Now it's time to get the word out!

Just imagine how cool it will be to see people wearing something that started as a design in your sketchbook. Now picture it happening in Paris, Tokyo...even Singapore. Hey, why not? You want as many people as possible wearing your creations!

So, how do you get there? There are three main steps in the business of fashion: branding (coming up with a name), promotion (spreading the word), and selling (actually getting your clothes into a store). And how can you make your business approach as creative and original as your designs? Consider it a challenge: think big!

A Canadian fashion designer named Rita Liefhebber rented a Mack truck, cleaned out the back, stocked it with her latest collection, and drove it around during New York Fashion Week, inviting editors to come in and check out her stuff. Her ingenuity got people talking—and won her a whole bunch of new fans!

The secret of promotion is to think of it as just another extension of your collection. You're spreading the word about something that you already deeply believe in. And you know what? Other people will believe in you, too! Inspired blog writers and store owners will help bring your message to the people.

Now let's do this!

Who Am I?

Your brand is more than just a name—it's basically your public identity. When people hear the name of your fashion line, you want them to immediately associate something with it. Like how you might think "minimalist" when you hear Calvin Klein… or even "Big Mac" when you hear McDonald's. Same deal!

STEP 1:
My Definition

Now you need to decide what you want those associations to be. Write down a bunch of words that define what your fashion line is all about. Is it elegant? Avant-garde? Rock 'n' roll? Does it involve drapery? Embellishment? Simplicity? Keep that list handy. It's a quick reference guide to the overall brand image you're working toward.

STEP 2:
Say my Name

Here's a fun thing to think about when you're doing the dishes or walking the dog: What should you name your fashion line? The standard designer practice is to use either your full name or your last name, but it's totally up to you! Feel free to get creative: Gwen Stefani called her fashion line L.A.M.B., in honor of her first solo album, *Love, Angel, Music, Baby.*

TIP: Just make sure you really love what you choose! The designers behind Proenza Schouler—who combined their mothers' maiden names to create the name of their line—said one of their biggest regrets is their name. It's too long and tricky to spell!

STEP 3:
Label Love

Next up: designing your logo! For inspiration, take a look at logos that already exist—of fashion labels, sure, but also of bands, magazines, the titles on book covers. Then type the name of your fashion line into a computer and change up the font. How does your perception of the name change with the fonts? Which one best embodies the words on your list? You can always hire a graphic designer to create a font that is 100% unique to you, but this easy test will give you a sense of which direction to head in!

BONUS STEP:
Branching Out

Once designers have established their brand, they often think about adding to it. They might design a shoe line, sunglasses, a fragrance—or all of those things and much more! You don't need to get sidetracked with those extras right now, but hey, it never hurts to have a big picture in mind! Maybe you can think of a way to branch out right now.

Staying on Message

All of the elements of a fashion line—from the collection to the name to the logo—need to be as consistent as possible. Why? When something veers away from what you've already established as your look, it confuses people. You wouldn't create a graffiti logo for a collection of cocktail dresses, just like you wouldn't choose flowing, handwritten script for your skate shoes logo. That doesn't mean you can't shake up expectations a little! Just remember: your branding should always reinforce your design message.

Getting Hands On

What do you do when you want to quickly find info on a band or a movie? You search the web, right?

People will want to surf for your fashion line, too, so you need to make sure that they can find you. As a bonus, taking advantage of technology is the easiest, quickest, and cheapest way of getting your name out there!

FASHION CENTRAL

Start by creating a website, which acts like a snapshot of your fashion line. Add all the basic info—when you started your line, what your line is all about—and then brainstorm ways that you can show off your clothes on the site. This is where it gets really interesting!

OLD SCHOOL—CREATE A LOOKBOOK

A lookbook is like a slideshow catalogue of your clothes: each photo shows a model wearing a different outfit from your latest collection—like a fashion show. Designers often keep it simple by sticking with one model, a white background, and straight-on photography so that the attention is squarely on the clothes. You can stick with this formula or add a little more to your setting—it's up to you!

NEW SCHOOL—MAKE A VIDEO

Fashion videos are increasingly popular, in part because they're so much fun to make. They can capture the spirit of your line and make people think, "Ooh, I want those pants!" A video's process is the same as that of a photo shoot—you find an idea, get your team together, and start shooting! It may be a picnic scene in the park with tea cups, pastel dresses, and afternoon light. Or how about your denim line seen downtown surrounded by steel skyscrapers? Endless options!

Note: A video is different from a shoot in two main ways:

1. *Music.* Essential for maximum effect! To use professional music, request permission from the band's record company. You'll have a better chance of getting a "Sure!" if you ask a band that isn't, you know, Coldplay.

2. *Editing.* You can usually download editing programs for free. Match the music to the shots as much as possible, and leave enough room at the end of the video to include credits for all the clothing you feature.

Now make the video viral! Post it on your site and on YouTube, and wait for the hits to come in!

LIKE WILDFIRE

These days, everything on the web is connected. Plugging into social media, like Facebook and Twitter, will only extend your reach. Use social media to tell people when you're hosting your next fashion show or to post behind-the-scenes pics of your fashion video. Just don't spread yourself too thin. Social media works best when you can devote enough time to one or two sites and help them grow. And get your parents' permission before you start up something on the web.

The Key to the Gates

What's the best thing about the rise of blogs and social media? Today, anyone can find a way to contribute to the world's fashion conversation.

> 66 Before the Internet, fashion was much more controlled. Now it's so easy for everyone—including teens—to share their voice, whether as bloggers or designers. The gargoyles at the gate keeping people out don't exist in the same way, which means that there's much more room for all kinds of creative people in fashion. 99
>
> —Kelly Cutrone
> **PUBLICIST**

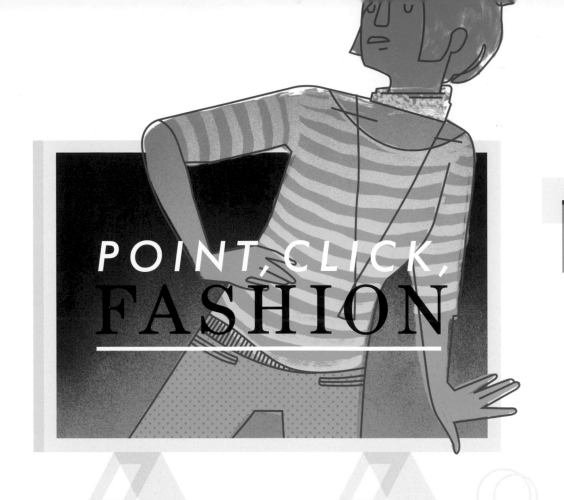

POINT, CLICK, FASHION

Starting a blog is another way for you to connect with potential fans. Blogs are more personal than websites, so you can let your personality shine through! But you don't need to be a designer, photographer, or any other type of professional to create a blog about fashion. That's one of the great things about them: blogs are for everybody.

ONE IN A MILLION

Of course, since anyone can start a blog, it can be hard to stand out. How do you make yours unique? Maybe you have a neat concept, like you're going to write a fashion-inspired haiku every day or you're planning solely to critique fashion magazines. No matter what your angle is, developing your writing and reporting skills will give you a major head start. Use proper grammar and spell-check, and most important, start thinking like a fashion journalist. Chances are you have the instincts already—you just need to build on them!

FASHION JOURNALISM:
A CRASH COURSE

1. READ UP ON YOUR INTERESTS

Keep track of what interests you the most: Do you love fashion photography? Street style? Designers like Coco Chanel? There isn't any right answer, but figuring out what you like best will help readers understand your blog's focus and add depth to your point of view.

2. BE A LEADER

The best fashion writers have their own ideas and opinions—they're the ones identifying trends and starting conversations that other people join. The more you research, the more you'll notice patterns in fashion. Maybe there was a lot of leopard print at the recent runway shows, or plaid shirts suddenly seem to be everywhere at your school. Don't wait for other people to comment on it. The ability to spot talent and trends early will always set you apart.

3. ALWAYS BE CURIOUS

Think of it as your fashion ABCs. Don't be afraid to leave your computer and head out into the neighborhood. If you notice that a new vintage shop opened up nearby, go in and check it out. If you want to know how long they've been open for, ask, even though you might be nervous at first. As tough as it is, it's worth the effort. You learn so much more when you talk to people, and the vast majority of them will be excited to tell you about themselves and what's new.

Tip: If you're going to start a blog, let your parents know. They don't have to be your number one readers, but they should be in the loop about everything that you're doing publicly on the Internet. You know the drill: safety first!

Be Brave

Sometimes to get the story—or the snapshot—you need to really put yourself out there. Take Tommy Ton, who started his blog, jakandjil.com, by just showing up at Paris Fashion Week and hanging around outside with his camera.

❝I took photos of the crowds, the fashion editors, the models. I was so scared—I was this totally nerdy kid around these incredibly glamorous people—but it was enthralling, too.❞

—Tommy Ton
PHOTOGRAPHER
JAKANDJIL.COM

Buying&Selling

The next time you go into a clothing shop, take an extra-long look around. It may seem as though everyone's job is totally obvious: there's the person behind the cash and the people helping the customers. Simple, right? But there's also a lot going on behind the scenes. This is the journey of how a dress might travel from a designer's studio to a store.

A The designer creates the dress in his or her studio.

B The designer displays the dress at a runway show. In the audience, among the fashion editors and bloggers, are buyers who work for stores like Saks Fifth Avenue. A buyer's job is to literally "buy" clothes from designers to sell at their stores. Not a bad gig!

C Now the buyer makes an appointment to visit the designer's showroom so he can check out the dress close up. ("Gorgeous!") Then he places an order for the dress on behalf of the store.

D The dress arrives at the store as part of a shipment.

E The store's creative director gets first dibs on what to do with the dress. The creative director usually oversees the window displays, and she might want to place the dress in the window to create a particular mood or help tell a story. Hmmm, maybe Cinderella?

F Now the fashion merchandiser steps in. His or her job is to find the best possible place to put the dress in the store so that it will sell, sell, sell!

G A customer comes in, takes one look at the dress, and says, "I can't live without it!" The journey is complete!

Hosting a Trunk Show

One day your clothes will be featured in the windows of Saks (believe it!), but when you're just starting out, a trunk show might be your best bet to sell your stuff. A trunk show is a special sale where you invite people over to your house to check out (and hopefully buy) pieces from your latest collection. Consider inviting a few designer friends to join you in selling and make an afternoon of it—the more the merrier!

Art of Attraction

Why do you walk right by one window display but stop and stare at another? The key to a great display is sparking people's imagination.

> 66 There's a magic to creating window displays—you want to give people a sense of joy and wonder. You start with the clothes and then go from there. It's all about creating an irresistible and inspiring mood. 99
>
> —John Gerhardt
> **AWARD-WINNING WINDOW DRESSER**

There you have it—what I've learned so far about the fashion world! The exciting thing is that there's always, always more to learn. If you're at the stage where you're raring to go, read on! I've assembled toolkits for aspiring designers, photographers, stylists, editors (and interns!) that will help you plan out your next steps. But if you want to chill and digest the info you've already read, I can relate.

After getting swept up in fashion as a young teen, I fell away from it for a little while and got more into music, movies, and books. When I got back into it about five years later, I found that my new knowledge about people like Patti Smith, Woody Allen, and F. Scott Fitzgerald actually helped me understand and appreciate fashion that much more. Fashion will always be there for you when you decide that you're ready for it.

I can't wait to see what you bring to the world!

THE STYLE FILES

Ready to take what you've learned and bring it to the next level? The following pages showcase items and ideas that can help you get there. Think of it as your fashion starter kit!

DESIGNER ESSENTIALS
Making the Magic Happen

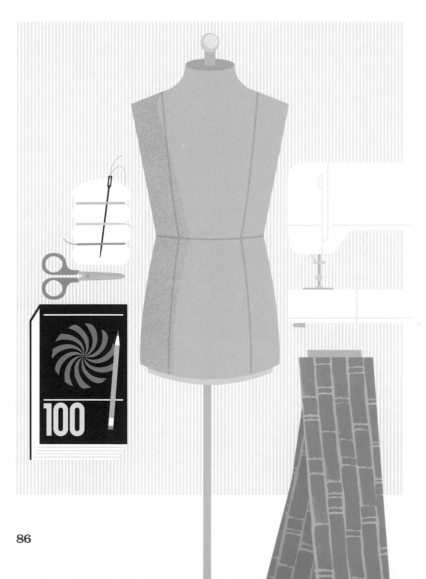

By now, you know that the most important thing a designer needs to get started is curiosity: about fashion, people, and the world that he or she lives in. But it's also a good idea to have a few items that can help turn that curiosity into clothes! Here are seven things that will help all aspiring designers transform their ideas into reality.

A work space: Having a dedicated area to design and create clothes will make you feel more like a "real" designer, even if, for now, it's just your basement. No matter. Make the space as "you" as possible, with your music, your inspiration board, and the following things:

A sketch pad: Before you start threading your needle, get all your amazing ideas down on paper. This will give you something specific to work from, which will help keep you on track. Your sketches will also keep your excitement levels up—you can keep glancing at how great the final result will be!

A judy: A judy is like a mannequin, except with more realistic measurements—and, um, without the head. Designers drape material around it as a substitute for an actual person. Ask an adult to help you track down a judy—you can often find used ones in classified ads or on Craigslist. In the meantime, you can always ask your best friend to be your judy (just watch those pins!).

A sewing kit: Just the basics: needles, spools of thread, and scissors—preferably fabric scissors, which cut through fabric much more smoothly than the regular scissors in your kitchen drawer.

A sewing machine: You can always sew by hand (which means using just a needle and thread), but a sewing machine will be more precise and make the work go much, much faster. You'll be able to create more in less time!

A fashion dictionary: Seriously! Fashion has literally hundreds of its own words, so it's very handy to have a reference book that you can turn to when you come across a word you don't know—or one that you can never seem to remember. I'm that way with "Romper: (n) a one-piece garment with the lower part shaped like loose-fitting shorts." Thanks, dictionary!

Fabric: You'll have a sense from your sketches what kind of fabric you want to use—cotton, flannel, lace—and in what colors. Visit your local fabric store and poke around. You might discover an incredible print or pattern that will take your design to the next level! You can also take apart old clothes that you don't wear anymore and use them to create something new.

> 66 I picked up my interest in sewing from my mom. I started making clothes from fabrics around the house, and one day she took me to the fabric store to get some new fabrics to work with. The first thing I ever made for myself was a pair of sky-blue-and-white-plaid pants. 99
>
> —Jeremy Laing
> **FASHION DESIGNER**

PHOTOGRAPHER ESSENTIALS
The Big Picture

These days, it can seem like everyone is a photographer. But even though it's easier than ever before to take and share pictures, being a great photographer is as challenging now as it ever was.

More than anyone else in fashion, photographers use a lot of specialty equipment. (Tip: add a photo assistant to your wish list!) Equipment can be pricey, so start with the basics—like a camera—and work your way up to the more complicated stuff. And remember: the two most essential things for any photographer—instinct and a good eye—don't cost a thing.

Camera: Digital cameras are amazing because they give you the freedom to experiment and snap away. You can take as many photos as you like! If you prefer the look that film or Polaroid cameras give photos, check out eBay, an excellent resource for used cameras.

Lenses: A lens fastens onto your camera's shutter, and changes the look and feel of each shot. Wide-angle lenses, which (yep) capture a wider view, are great for landscapes. Telephoto lenses isolate the subject from the background, making them perfect for portraits and candid street-style snaps.

Lights and reflectors: These do exactly what their names suggest—they lighten up a shot or softly reflect light onto the subjects in the picture. Lights can be super bulky, but reflectors fold up to be about the size of a magazine.

Music: Good tunes will keep everyone's energy up on a shoot, including yours. Music can also create atmosphere: put on some heavy Beethoven for moody moments and Rihanna when you want to lighten things up!

Grease pencil and film loupe: These are essentials if you're using film, not digital. The pencil is for circling your favorite photos from a shoot. Rub off the pencil as you make your final decisions: "This one! No, this one is perfect. Wait, this one is nice, too…" A film loupe is like a magnifying glass that allows you to examine photos very closely to spot any imperfections.

Laptop: You can check out your pics, resize them, and send them to friends or to the art director at a magazine. You can also retouch them, which means getting rid of flaws like red eyes, stray hairs, or mysterious mustard stains.

> **66** I've been a professional photographer for 15 years, and the digital revolution in photography has changed everything. Shoots are so much faster—and less nerve-wracking—because the immediacy means you can see right away which props and poses are working best.**99**
>
> —Chris Chapman
> **FASHION PHOTOGRAPHER**

STYLIST ESSENTIALS
More Than Playing Dress-up

You know those makeover shows on TV, where experts help someone totally transform his or her wardrobe? It's like playing dress-up with purpose—this is your first task as an aspiring stylist. Get a friend to be your "model" (or be your own), then come up with a look that you want to create. How about punk or glam? Now use clothes and accessories to match the look in your head to the look on your model.

When you're first learning to style, your closet will probably be your main resource. But when professional stylists are on the job, they need a few extra things to make sure that they—and the people they're styling—are well dressed from head to toe.

Magazines: For inspiration! Stylists are like encyclopedias when it comes to magazines because they flip through so many of them. Magazines also help them keep up to date on new designers and shops worth checking out.

Clips and pins: The final shot has to look perfect, but it takes a lot of work to make it that way. The clips and pins help fake it a little by pinching and cinching loose bits so that clothes fit exactly right.

Tape: Duct tape, in particular. Stylists tape the bottom of shoes to prevent them from getting all scuffed up on fashion shoots. Double-sided tape also helps with hemlines. Want to adjust the length of a skirt? Tuck it under and tape it. Presto, a new look!

Steamer: Think of it as your household iron on multivitamins. The hot steam immediately relaxes wrinkles without directly touching the fabric, so there is less chance of damage. Make a combined Christmas and birthday list, and put a steamer at the top!

Comfy shoes: Though it might be tempting to try to be as glamorous as the models they dress, stylists tend to stay as comfortable as possible while they're out "pulling"—that's fashion lingo for collecting all the clothes and accessories for a shoot.

Emergency kit: Scissors to snip stray threads, glue in case a high heel breaks—better to have them with you than be forced to run to the corner store with the clock ticking!

> 66 You never know what's going to happen on a shoot, so you have to be prepared for everything. I always make sure to pack a needle and thread in every color. 99
>
> —Phillip Bloch
> **CELEBRITY STYLIST**

MAGAZINE ESSENTIALS
Smells Like Team Spirit

The path to being a great writer, editor, or art director is a hard one requiring lots of skill and knowledge. Starting a blog is a good way to kick off your journey: you'll be able to try everything from choosing the design and fonts to coming up with story ideas and writing. That kind of practical experience will take you a long way.

But you know what else will help? Joining a baseball team or a dance committee. Seriously. Why? You'll learn the value of teamwork. All kinds of creative people work at fashion magazines: writers, designers, fashion and beauty editors. With so many different types of people, your top must-have is a spirit of collaboration. Of course, these bits and pieces will help, too!

Pens and red pen: Add pens to every bag you own and keep a stockpile at your desk so that you're never without one. (You don't want to be the journalist asking, "Um, can I borrow that?") When you're proofreading stories for errors, a red pen is handy to make your comments stand out: "Explain, please! Cut this sentence! Great job!"

Digital recorder: Digital files are like a security blanket. You can access them anytime and they'll capture quotes with perfect accuracy. It's still a good idea to take notes during interviews just in case there's a tech blip—it's happened to me, and it's brutal!

Calendar: In magazines, you usually work about three months ahead of the publication date (so in December, you'll be finishing up your March issue). A calendar, whether on your computer or a bulletin board, helps you keep track of the production timeline so you can get the issue out on time.

Day planner: You'll also have lots of day-to-day commitments to organize: events, story meetings, photo shoots. A daily planner helps keep everything in one place—a big help when you're always on the go!

> 66 I always recommend that people read Grace Mirabella's autobiography, *In & Out of Vogue*. She was the editor of *Vogue* at an important time in North American fashion—between editors Diana Vreeland and Anna Wintour and during the rise of the American working woman's wardrobe. She's a hero of mine. 99
>
> —Nathalie Atkinson
> **FASHION JOURNALIST**

Phone: Email—fast, easy, but impersonal—rules the communication world. However, the personal touch of a phone call can go a long way to forming a connection with someone, whether it's a PR rep or an interview subject.

Books: Photography and art books are amazing references and a source of inspiration for photo shoots. Reading biographies of famous editors and art directors—and learning how they achieved their dreams—will help fuel your own fire!

INTERN ESSENTIALS
Great Expectations

Almost everyone who ends up working in fashion starts out by taking an internship of some kind—which means working for free (or very little) while you learn and gain experience. Young designers often apprentice with established designers; stylists and photographers assist more experienced counterparts; would-be editors and art directors intern at newspapers or magazines.

A word about working for free: Internships can be tough, but they're also a fascinating window into the realities of the fashion world. You might help with research, organize a closet of fashion samples, or even just order lunch during a photo shoot. Whatever the specifics of your internship, your real job is to excel. Your first internship might be years away, but learning a few tools and tricks of the trade now will help you knock it out of the park when your chance comes!

A notebook: People will be explaining things from the moment you walk in the door. Write down as much as you can, or use a digital tape recorder. You'll learn so much so quickly and you'll need to hold on to that info—by noon, you don't want to be wondering if your boss said to research the style of designer Pierre Cardin…or designer Pierre Balmain! If you still miss something, don't stress—just ask! It's so much better to clear up any confusion than to just guess…and guess wrong.

Water and healthy snacks: One of the best ways to impress your boss? An amazing work ethic. Internships are usually three or four months, so they're like a really long job interview. Get there early and stay late! Staying hydrated will help keep you focused, and a stockpile of snacks will come in handy if you suddenly need to work through lunch.

Library card and bus or subway pass: Interns need to be ready to do whatever their boss asks them, including hopping on the subway to pick up clothing samples, an art book from the library downtown, or a low-fat, half-caf latte (extra hot!).

Sensible clothes: The interns swishing around on TV in towering high heels can look more like models before a runway show than office workers. Since you'll (likely) be working crazy hours and (possibly) zipping all over town, wear stylish clothes that are also comfortable, so you both represent your team well and don't end up with fashion-related injuries by day two!

A good attitude: The absolute, 100% most important tool. Interns are on the bottom rung of the ladder—hey, someone has to be! So, be prepared to grin and bear it while you're learning everything you can.

> **"** I've driven vans, made deliveries all over the city, cleaned the floor. Did I love it? No! But I learned from it, and that hard work has made me appreciate my design career that much more. **"**
>
> —Giles Deacon
> **FASHION DESIGNER**
> *GILES AND UNGARO*

Head to Toe 🔍

A SPECIAL FASHION INDEX FOR YOU TO USE

Last look: I've been lucky to work with amazingly talented people during my magazine career; my thanks to all of them and special thanks to David Livingstone for giving me my start. Thanks to the following lovely group for their interview time: Nathalie Atkinson, Philip Bloch, Leith Clark, Kelly Cutrone, Giles Deacon, Calla Haynes, Michael Kors, Jeremy Laing, Crystal Renn, Coco Rocha, Jonathan Saunders, and Tommy Ton. Thanks to Emily Blake and Jennifer Lee for all their support. Major thanks to Jeff Kulak, my illustrator/designer, who knows a thing or two about WOW factor, and especially to my incredible editor, John Crossingham, for his wit but mostly his wisdom.